An Introduction
to the Old English Language
and its Literature

Stephen Pollington

Anglo-Saxon Books

By the same Author

Leechcraft – Early English Charms, Plantlore and Healing
The English Warrior: from earliest times to 1066
Wordcraft: Concise Dictionary and Thesaurus
First Steps in Old English
Rudiments of Runelore
The Warrior's Way

First Published 1994
Revised, Expanded and Reprinted 1996
Reprinted 1999
Reprinted 2001

Published by
Anglo-Saxon Books
Frithgarth
Thetford Forest Park
Hockwold-cum-Wilton
Norfolk England

Printed by
Antony Rowe Ltd
Chippenham
Wiltshire England

British Library Cataloguing-in-Publication Data. A catalogue record for this book is available from the British Library.

ISBN 1–898281–06–8

Contents

Introduction to the Second Edition

The first edition of this booklet was intended as a brief introduction to the subject – the earliest history of the English language and the various writings in those ancient versions of it – adapted from a talk I gave to a meeting of Þa Engliscan Gesiþas (The English Companions) in February 1994. The work has proven useful and popular, and has served as a handy thumbnail sketch for many who have gone on to study the language in greater detail. For this reason, when the time came for consideration of a reprint, I was particularly concerned to add in some additional material which I felt would serve to guide those wishing to know more, and to correct a few typographical errors which had crept into the original.

The value of a work such as this is that it should be accessible to people with no specialist knowledge in the subject – either newcomers wishing for some guidance before going on to pursue their specific interest, or those who merely want outline information for reference. I hope to have included enough for both groups of what they need, but no doubt many will feel that there are omissions of useful material.

The texts referred to are mostly given in translation, although there is a small section demonstrating how the original language works for those who wish to follow this up. The literary quality of these translations (all my own) is variable, being intended to illustrate the range of material in Old English and to stay reasonably faithful to the original texts. Nevertheless, I hope to whet a few appetites, or issue a challenge to do better!

My thanks are due to those readers of the first edition who have conveyed to me their reactions to it, and to Tony and Pearl Linsell of *Anglo-Saxon Books* for giving me the opportunity to produce what I hope is a substantially different booklet. One rarely gets a second bite at the cherry!

Steve Pollington,
Essex, 1996

An Introduction to the Old English Language and its Literature

This book is a general introduction to Old English (OE) and I apologise in advance for writing about what some readers will already know. What I propose to do here is to look at three things:

1. Some misconceptions about Old English.
2. The grammar, with some examples of Old English in action.
3. What sorts of things were written in the language.

Some Misconceptions

Before proceeding to look at what Old English (OE) is like in detail, it might be helpful to look at three things that people think it is like.

First, because OE is sometimes called 'Anglo-Saxon', and furthermore because this term is used in some circles to mean foul language – swearing and cursing, or if you prefer, effing and blinding – the idea has some currency that OE is synonymous with strong and vulgar speech. Now, as a regular and practised user of this section of our vocabulary, I have looked into this matter with my other hat on (that is, of philologist) and I have to disappoint you by saying that of the whole range of about twenty 'unacceptable' words in current use, only half a dozen have any claim to be Old English. Perhaps the misconception arises from the fact that the words for most parts of the body and many of the more basic human activities are OE in origin: everything from 'head' to 'toe', from 'eat' and 'drink' to 'see' and 'hear', 'wake' and 'sleep'. The association of the language with these down-to-earth aspects of life reflects the cultural and social history of the English people, their absorption of Viking settlers from whom they borrowed many homely words (like 'law', 'husband' and 'sky') and their eventual domination by Norman aristocrats whose vocabulary, when it entered English, did so at the upper end of the social scale. For example, a 'table' or 'chair' is a nobler piece of furniture than a 'board' or 'stool' – and of course, both the latter are the Old English words (*bord* and *stōl*) for these items. A further and rather telling example is the fact that the English words for many animals (such as 'cow', 'sheep', 'boar', 'deer') refer to the living creature in the hands of the farmer or herdsman, while once slaughtered, cooked and served to the Norman barony they acquire a French-based culinary name: 'beef', 'mutton', 'pork' or 'venison'.

Another idea I sometimes hear, particularly from people with only memories of language learning from their schooldays, is that OE is very complicated with lots of endings on the words, like French or Latin. This is highly subjective, of course: it depends what you are comparing OE with as to how complicated you will think it is. But to set the record straight, it is worth stating that there are changing word endings (called *inflexions*) in OE just as there are in our modern language. Yet OE was never as involved as Latin; it is a much more "modern " language with about the same degree of change as we find in modern German or Dutch.

Anyone who has studied French knows that there are separate sets of verb stems and endings to show tense:

he is	–	*il est*
he will be	–	*il sera*
he would be	–	*il serait*
he was	–	*il était* or *il fut*

as well as the compound tenses such as 'has been', 'had been', 'would have been', etc. OE is much more pragmatic about all this, as I shall show later on, and instead of using five different tenses it only has two: past and 'non-past' or present. There is no future tense in OE – it may surprise you to know that there is no future tense in New English (NE) either! By which I mean that there is no way of indicating simple futurity as the French do with *il sera*. We can say that something 'is going' to happen but that is a present process (using 'is') or that it 'will' happen but that only discloses an intention. There is always some other shade of meaning involved when we discuss the future in English, modern or Old.

In the matter of nouns, there is a suspicion that OE has a system like that in Latin whereby there are lots of endings according to the word's function in the sentence. Now this is partly true, since both Latin and OE share a common ancestry, but our language has rationalized to some

8

extent so that instead of having potentially twelve endings (as a Latin noun has) the OE one has only eight. But no Latin noun actually has twelve <u>different</u> endings because they tend to double up – *puellae* means both 'girls' and 'of a girl'. The most any single noun has, as far as I am aware, is nine separate endings, while for comparison out of a possible eight endings, OE nouns have between three (*sunu*) and six (*stān*), the largest single group having four (the weak nouns). But modern English nouns still have four endings:

child	children	child's	children's
son	sons	son's	sons'

so again the modern and ancient forms of our language are of comparable complexity.

There is no doubt that Latin is more involved, more complicated and more of a memory test than OE, but thousands of people learn it who would think our language too difficult. This is entirely illogical, and reflects the low status our English heritage currently has – to be of value, things have to be imported, borrowed from alien cultures.

When people see or hear a passage of OE and particularly if they pick up a grammar or students' reader cold, they often remark that it is 'just like German'. There is some truth in this statement, but it is not the whole story and it certainly doesn't mean that if you want to learn OE you must first learn modern German. (The German language is a subject in itself, and is not directly relevant to the study of OE. Anyone who already knows some German may occasionally find it helpful, but you don't really need to know anything but English to succeed in mastering the ancient form of the language.) But Old English like German, Dutch, the Scandinavian languages, Icelandic and Faroese is part of a single language family – all these various languages' ancestors converge into a single original language ('proto-language') which for want of a better name we call Proto-Germanic and which was already spoken on the Baltic and North West Continent around the time of Christ.

In pronunciation, the OE word spelt s-t-ā-n is closer to English 'stone' than German 'Stein' and 'speech' is *spræc* not *Sprach*. Many of the characteristic sounds of 'official' German (*Hochdeutsch*) are due to the so-called *zweite Lautverschiebung* or 'second sound-shift' which made, for example, an original (found in English) 't' into German 'ts' (spelt *z*). It is interesting and illuminating to pick up correspondences in the two languages: many of you will know the German word *zimmer* (a room) which you can then relate to the OE *timrian* (to build) and our word 'timber', wood for building with. These correspondences take on a fascination of their own: work out why the Germans say *klein* meaning 'small' and we say 'clean', or they say *zaun* meaning 'hedge' and we say 'town'.

So, having demonstrated, I hope, that OE is not merely abusive language, is not intrinsically difficult and not merely a dialect of German, it is fair to ask two questions: 'What is Old English?' and 'Why would anyone bother to learn it?'

What is 'Old English'?

'What is OE?' can be simply answered: it is the speech of the English from the earliest recorded times up to the completion of the changes which produced the language we call Middle English (ME). This doesn't get us very far towards a definition, so let's just say that English is probably first recorded as place-names in Latin charters granting land to the church and the earliest of these known to survive is dated to 692 AD – about thirteen hundred years ago, if the dating is sound. This text, granting lands east of London to Barking Abbey, may not be the oldest English text, however: before the church arrived in 597 and for at least two centuries afterwards, Englishmen used an older script to write in – the runes, subject of much speculation and antiquarian enquiry ever since. Possibly the oldest English text is a coin from between c.450 to 500 AD bearing the legend:

S C A N O M O D U

a male personal name *Scanōmōdu*. This text is definitely of North Sea Germanic type as the second and third characters have a distinctive

10

shape, but it is so early that it could be either early English or Frisian, a related language from the coast of the Netherlands. In other words, the linguistic form here is so ancient it belongs to a time before there was any distinction between English and Flemish, as the languages both come from a common source. (Incidentally this name would appear later in West Saxon as *Sceanmōd.*)

The ancestor of the English language was brought here by troops serving first in the Roman army, and subsequently with the post-Roman British authorities. After the upheavals and strife of the fifth century, some form of Germanic speech was the normal form of communication along the eastern seaboard of Britain, having replaced both British (what would later become Welsh) and Vulgar Latin, the everyday means of communication throughout the Roman Empire. We can tell that this change took place rapidly and completely by the virtual wholesale replacement of British place-names by English ones – even though many rivers retain their former titles, such as 'Thames', there is hardly a pre-English place-name in the southern and eastern parts of the country[1]. As conquest followed conquest, the English-speaking, English-held lands extended further west and north – the later the adoption of English speech, the greater the survival of British place-names. Western Cornwall held out till the tenth century as a separate polity and so there English names are in a minority.

At the other end of the OE period, the language continued to be written up to about 1150 AD, although its spelling had altered already at that date to reflect changes which had even then begun to transform it into Middle English (ME). English ceased to be written for about two centuries, and by the time it came back into favour it was in a very different guise. But that's another story.

Old English, then, is a Germanic language brought to these shores late in the Roman period and which was finally transformed some seven centuries later by a large influx of extraneous vocabulary and internal processes of re-organization. The new vocabulary came from the

---

[1] Those cities which survived the economic decline of the 5th century retain their Roman names (e.g. London/*Londinium*, Lincoln/*Lindum Colonia*) often with an English ending (Gloucester/*Glevum* + *ceaster* 'fort').

Norman élite, whose way of life reflected very different concerns from those of the disenfranchized English population. In fairness, though, the Scandinavian Norse influence was more probably the cause of the far-reaching changes in the structure of English. Old Norse – also a Germanic language – was fairly well comprehensible to English speakers and vice-versa. The main differences between Old Norse and Old English were not in the words themselves but in their endings. I have contrasted some English and Norse examples:

Modern English	Old English	Old Norse
a child	*bearn*	*barn*
of a child	*bearnes*	*barns*
the child	*ðæt bearn*	*barnit*
a man	*guma*	*gumi*
of a man	*guman*	*guma*
the man	*se guma*	*guminn*
a book	*bōc*	*bók*
of a book	*bēc*	*bókar*
the book	*sēo bōc*	*bókin*

Where English speakers met Norse speakers, the easiest thing to do to simplify communication was to drop the word-endings and rely on word order to get the meaning across. It was this process of fixed word order and fewer endings that has given rise to our modern language.

A short sentence from Old Norse and, below it, how it would have looked in Old English:

Eptir hann var konungr í Englandi son hans Játvarðr
'After him was king in England son of him Edward'

Æfter him wæs his sunu Eadweard cyning on Englalande
'After him was his son Edward king on England'

Dialects of Old English

Although for the purposes of this booklet I treat Old English as if it were one language, it consists in fact of at least four major dialects:

West Saxon spoken in the central southern counties and the west country;

South-eastern (or **Kentish**) spoken in the south east;

Mercian spoken in the Midlands;

Northumbrian spoken in the modern areas of northen England and lowland Scotland (say, from the Humber to Edinburgh).

Although 'Lallans' (Lowland Scots dialect) has often been considered as separate from other English dialects, this is simply because of the later historical political division – the Scots tongue is a descendant of OE just as much as the standard English of the south.

Mercian and Northumbrian are collectively known as **Anglian**, because of certain shared features (e.g. their treatment of certain vowels). The dialect groupings have a large 'grey area' in the East Midlands and East Anglia where we simply don't have enough evidence to be certain quite what the local dialect was like. Both these areas were later subject to heavy Scandinavian influence, so the usual fall-backs such as place-names and personal names are not as helpful as they might otherwise be. Similarly, although there are a few early records with names of places and people in, the dialects of distinct regions such as the kingdoms of the South Saxons (modern Sussex), the East Saxons (modern Essex, Hertfordshire, Surrey, Middlesex and western Kent) or the *Wihtware* (modern Isle of Wight and Solent estuary) are very difficult to study.

Generally speaking, students of Old English are encouraged to begin with West Saxon since it is in this particular variant that the greater part of the literature that survives has been recorded. West Saxon has two distinct periods: the 'early' (eWS) dating from the ninth century – the time of Alfred; and the 'late' (lWS) from about the mid-tenth century on. There are variations in spelling between the two periods, and most grammars lean towards the earlier forms.

13

Writing and Spelling

Of course, OE doesn't look much like what we now recognize as English, in either its own lettering or in our modern printed versions, but I hope to show that we can overcome this. Here is a reconstruction of how one text would have looked and below that the edited text one would find in a printed version (see page 46 for the NE translation):

Example – Riddle 47 from the Exeter Book

Moððe poɲð ꝼɲæꞇ. Me þæꞇ þuhꞇe pɲæꞇlicu pẏɲð, þa ic ꝥ punðoɲ ȝeꝼɲæȝn, þæꞇ ꞅe pẏɲm ꝼoɲꞅpealȝ peɲa ȝieð ꞃumeꞅ, þeoꝼ in þẏꞅꞇɲo þɲẏmꝼæꞅꞇne cpiðe ⁊ þæꞅ ꞅꞇɲanȝen ꞅꞇaþol. ꞅꞇælȝieꞃꞇ ne pæꞅ pihꞇe þẏ ȝleapɲa, þe he þam poɲðum ꞅpealȝ.

Moððe word frǣt. Mē þæt þūhte wrǣtlicu wyrd, þā ic þæt wundor gefrǣgn, þæt se wyrm forswealg wera gied sumes, þēof in þȳstro þrymfæstne cwide and þæs strangan staþol. Stælgiest ne wæs wihte þȳ glēawra, þe hē þām wordum swealg.

For those of you who have never seen a page of OE before, or opened a grammar, I will give you an idea of how it works in practice. First the spelling: here are a few OE words which you may not recognize immediately.

bodig	body	*-ig* pronounced '-ee'
sceanca	shank (leg)	*sce-* pronounced 'sh-'
cnēo	knee	still pronouncing the 'k'
tā	toe	
fōt	foot	
anclēow	ankle	
hype	hip	two syllables: hy – pe
þēoh	thigh	*þ* = th

14

brēost	breast, chest	
earm	arm	
hand	hand	
finger	finger	
wrist	wrist	still pronouncing the 'w'
elnboga	elbow	(*eln* forearm + *boga* bend)
nosu	nose	
cinn	chin	*ci-* pronounced 'chi-'
ēare	ear	two syllables: ea -re
ēage	eye	*-ge* pronounced '-ye'
brū	brow	pronounced like 'brew'

You can see that the main parts of the words are pretty much identical to ours and it's mainly the endings which have been dropped – remember that mixing with speakers of Old Norse was probably responsible for this. You should also note that every letter is pronounced, and that there are certain special letters like 'thorn' (þ), the *th* in 'thigh'. There are combinations of sounds which are unfamiliar now, but generally when you hear the words pronounced they are recognisably English.

The finer details of Old English spelling are a large and complex subject, and variations in the practice can help us to locate the probable origins of texts by carefully evaluating all the clues. For example, there was a tendency in Northumbrian not to pronounce the final *-n* of certain types of words (notably weak nouns, numerals and verbal infinitives) so that if a scribe spells the word *seofon* 'seven' as *seofo*, then this will be taken as an indication of possible Northumbrian origin for the text. The more consistent the features are, the less likely that they can be put down to chance or scribal misunderstanding, and so the greater the likelihood of the text having been written in that area.

Anglo-Saxon scribes used a modified form of the Roman alphabet which was common in the British Isles (hence its name, 'insular') and may have been taught by Irish missionaries. The Roman characters were not a perfect match for the characteristics of the English language (then or now), however, and there were many problems in representing the full range of sounds through the limited set of letters. But the English did have experience of writing in runes, where they had simply invented new characters to cover new sounds, and they applied this principle to the Latin letters. They introduced two runes into the bookhand: þ for the sounds we write 'th' (as in 'this' and 'thin') and Ƿ for the sound we write as 'w'; previously these had been written 'th' and 'uu' respectively. They also introduced a variant of 'd' in the form 'Ð, ð' which alternates quite freely with 'þ', so that scribes will write the word 'this' as '*þis*' or '*ðis*' almost indiscriminately according to personal preference or whim.

The vowels proved especially tricky to record. The Roman character 'Æ, æ' was used to represent a front vowel half way between 'a' and 'e' (it is the vowel sound we find in 'cat', 'tap') and the slightly exotic letter 'y' (only used in Latin to spell Greek words) was adopted for a high front rounded vowel (not found in Standard English, but used on Merseyside in words like 'pool'; in French it is found in *tu, pu* and so on – an 'ee' sound pronounced with rounded lips). Old English also has a class of 'diphthongs' – vowels which start in one position and glide to another – which were spelt variously according to local dialect.

In time, a standardized spelling tradition was developed which must have helped enormously with reading documents produced elsewhere, or just very old ones. However there was never a fixed and formal spelling system such as we have today, and the impression of regularity given by modern edited texts is rather misleading. In fact, scribes were sometimes hesitant even about dividing up speech into words, and often a string of letters has to be teased apart into its constituents to try to recover the separate words.

Pronunciation

The following is only intended as a brief guide to an aggregate 'standard' reconstructed pronunciation. The welter of regional and chronological details are really only worth bothering with for the serious student.

Stress

Words in Old English are usually stressed on the first syllable, so that the name 'Alfred' has the same rhythm in OE as in NE. The major exception to this is the common prefix *ge-* which is never stressed so that the word *gesīþ* 'companion' is pronounced 'ye-SEEth'.

Consonants

The majority of Old English consonants are pronounced much as in the modern language; this applies to:–

b d l m n p t w

while the following are relatively rare and mostly used to spell foreign words:

k x z

and *j* and *q* were not used at all. The sound represented by *j* could be spelt *cg* (*brycg* 'bridge') and that by *q* with *cw* (*cweorn* 'quern, handmill'). The letter *v* was not differentiated from *u* at this time, nor *j* from *i*. Of the other consonants, most had different pronunciations depending what letters were next to them (much like to two *'c'*s in 'cat' and 'cello').

c	generally had the sound of 'k' (never of 's') – *camb* 'comb'; before *e* or *i* it had the sound of modern 'ch' – *cinn* 'chin'
h	at the beginning of a word was pronounced as now – *hāt* 'hot'; in the middle or at the end, it had the sound in Scottish 'loch' – *slōh* 'slew'
f	at the beginning or end of a word, was as in NE – *feoh* 'fee', *līf* 'life'; in the middle of a word it had the sound of modern 'v' – *seofon* 'seven'; when doubled it was as modern 'f' – *offrung* 'offering'
s	as with 'f', in first or last position or when doubled, as modern 's' – *seofon* 'seven', *lǣs* 'less', *prǣsse* 'army'; a single 's' in the middle of a word was as modern 'z' – *rīsan* 'rise'
þ, ð	these two letters both represent the same set of sounds, the 'th' of 'thin' and of 'this'; as with 'f' above, in first or last position or when doubled, they sound as 'thin' – *þorn* 'thorn', *bæð* 'bath', *smiþðe* 'smithy'; in the middle of a word, as in 'this' – *lāðan* 'loathe'
g	at the beginning of a word it has its modern sound – *gatu* 'gates'; in the middle or at the end of a word, it sounds like the sound in Scottish 'loch' – *sagu* 'saw', *bēag* 'ring'; before *e* or *i* the sound is of modern 'y' – *gield* 'yield', *geolu* 'yellow'

One of the things that makes Old English appear so very different from the modern language is the unfamiliar clusters of consonants, especially at the beginnings of words. Generally speaking, they just have to be pronounced as two sounds in sequence (*cnot* is just 'knot' with the 'k' pronounced, after all). The main exception to this is the group *sc(e)* which has the sound we spell 'sh' – *scip* 'ship', *scearp* 'sharp'.

Vowels

The vowels of Old English are a more complicated proposition since these sounds are the most fluid and therefore the hardest to capture in spelling. OE vowels are either 'long' or 'short'; conventionally, long vowels are marked with a macron (¯) and short vowels are left unmarked[2]. The following is a guide to their pronunciation:

	short	long
a	as in bud (southern English)	as in bard (no 'r')
æ	as in bat	as in bad
e	as in bed	as in bade
i	as in bid	as in bead
o	as in body	as in board (no 'r')
u	as in bull	as in booed
y	as in French *su*	as in French *sur*

The sounds of *y* can be made by saying the *i* sound, long or short, through rounded lips.

Diphthongs are vowels which start as one vowel and glide to become another – as the vowel of 'eye, I' starts as 'a' and moves towards 'i'. The OE ones are especially tricky, but here is an indication:

---

[2] Older editions of Old English works usually leave out any marks for vowel length because the Anglo-Saxon scribes did not put them into the originals. Students' editions and some other text books always include the macron over long vowels. Increasingly, in modern works vowel length is now found marked even in formal editions of texts.

ea   something like the sound in bared (no 'r') – moving from the 'bed' vowel to the back of the mouth

eo   similar to *ea* but moving to the front of the mouth not the back

ie   something like the sound in beard (no 'r') – moving from the 'bid' vowel downwards

io   similar to *ie* but moving to the front of the mouth as well as down

All diphthongs have both long and short variants.

Word Patterns

Inflexions, as I said above, are the patterns of changing endings which show a word's relationship to others in the sentence. Generally, nouns – the names of things and ideas, such as 'table', 'cushion', 'honesty' as well as places and people – show relationship to other nouns, as well as number ('stone' versus 'stones'). Adjectives – words which describe or qualify nouns, such as 'hollow', 'vague' or 'ramshackle' – tend to have endings which follow those of the nouns with which they are linked. Verbs – actions and states, such as 'drink', 'fall' or 'appear' – usually show number and tense: 'the building stands', 'the buildings stand', 'the empire fell'.

Let's look at some of these word endings I've mentioned. There are about a dozen different patterns of inflexion for nouns in OE, but there are only four principal ones. They fall into two groups – strong and weak – and have three genders, like Latin – masculine, feminine and neuter. If this sounds complicated, bear in mind that in NE we still have 'he', 'she' and 'it' which are remnants of this system. In brief, the strong masculines and neuters follow one pattern and the feminines another, while all the weak nouns follow a third. As an example, I have set out the nominative and genitive singular of some common nouns.

STRONG	Nominative		Genitive	
masculine	*mann*	a man	*mannes*	a man's
neuter	*scip*	a ship	*scipes*	a ship's
feminine	*cwēn*	a queen	*cwēne*	a queen's

WEAK	Nominative		Genitive	
masculine	*boda*	a messenger	*bodan*	a messenger's
neuter	*ēage*	an eye	*ēagan*	an eye's
feminine	*nunne*	a nun	*nunnan*	a nun's

If you can learn the individual forms of these six nouns off by heart, the remainder are just details which you will soon pick up once you begin reading the language.

The words for 'the/that' and 'this' also vary according to the gender – just like 'he, she, it' – and also with the word's function, so that the genitive *-s* ending of the masculine and neuter carries over into the word for 'the', for example, 'of the man' is *þæs mannes* and 'of the eye' is *þæs eagan*; but for the feminine there is a different form of 'the': *þǣre cwēne*. If you think of 'his' and 'its' (masculine and neuter) ending in *-s* and 'her' (feminine) ending in *-r* you can see how we have inherited the ghost of this system.

OE adjectives behave similarly, so that 'of a good man' is *gōdes mannes* and so on. They also have comparative forms like our modern ones – *cēne, cēnra, cēnest* (keen, keener, keenest) and our oddities like *gōd, betera, betst* (good, better, best).

The numbers are spelt differently but the series is still recognizable:

ān, twēgen, ðrīe, fēower, fīf, siex, seofon, eahta, nigon, tīen, endlufon, twelf.

No surprise, then, to find *twintig, ðrītig* and *hund, þūsund.* '*Hund*' is the word for 'hundred' and the '-red' was added later – it is actually a word meaning ' counting' so that 'hundred' is 'the counting of *hund.*'

The prepositions are also pretty familiar – words such as:

for, wið, to, æt, andlang, æfter, fram.

In French, or Spanish, or Italian, the English-speaker encounters the greatest problems with the verbs and their multitude of tenses, but the OE system is very economical: there are three main types of verb, called weak, strong and preterite-present and they are all well represented in the modern language.

Weak verbs form their past mostly with '-d-':

ic lifede	I lived
ic lufode	I loved
ic sǣde	I said
ic wolde	I would

For ease of pronunciation, some verbs substitute a '-t-' for '-d-':

ic sōhte	I sought
ic ðōhte	I thought
ic cyste	I kissed
ic sette	I set

These are the most numerous verbs in OE and have largely taken over today, so that all new coinings follow the weak pattern. Therefore when we invent a new activity such as 'computerize' the past tense is given as 'he computerized these records' on the model of 'devise:devised', not 'he computeroze these records' on the model of 'rise:rose'.

Strong verbs, in contrast, are few but make up the commonest activities. They form their past by changing the vowel according to a regular pattern:

ic singe	I sing
ic sang	I sang
ic hæbbe gesungen	I have sung

There are still a few different patterns:

drive	*drove*	*driven*
speak	*spoke*	*spoken*
eat	*ate*	*eaten*
bind	*bound*	*bound*
strike	*struck*	*struck*
hide	*hid*	*hidden*

and in OE there are more, because some words which are now weak verbs were then strong – 'help', for example, used to have a past tense *hulpon* but now we use the weak form 'helped'. You can observe this change at work currently in the fairly rare verbs 'thrive' and 'strive'. These historically follow the strong pattern ('throve; strove' and 'thriven; striven') but increasingly they are remodelled as weak verbs with 'thrived; strived'. However, for words in common use the pattern of rhyme is so strong that in the mouths of the uneducated 'bring' has a past tense 'brung'.

Preterite–present verbs are a small but very important group mainly used to express shades of meaning with other verbs. They are characterized in Modern English by not adding '-s' in the present ('he must', not 'he musts'). The commonest now are: can, may, must, will, need, shall, dare. Many of these behave likewise in OE, where there are a few more which have fallen out of use, such as *witan* 'to know' and *þurfan* 'to need'.

The word order of OE is generally freer than in our language, excepting poetry, where we allow greater freedom of word order – though curiously Anglo-Saxon poets' language was stricter than normal speech. However, the later a text was written, the more likely it is to conform to SVO (that is, subject-verb-object) word order. This is probably due to the development of a fixed literary style relying for effect on stylistic devices such as the reversal of expected elements in the sentence. Relatively tight rules of word order were necessary before the erosion of word endings could take place.

To give you a picture of OE in action, I have dissected a sentence from one of King Alfred's works – the translation he made of Boethius's treatise *De Consolatione Philosophiae* (On the Consolation of Philosophy) which he termed *Frōforbōc* (Comfort-book).

Þæt	*is*	*nu*	*hraþost*	*to secganne*
pronoun neuter nominative singular	verb 3rd singular present indicative	adverb	adverb	verbal infinitive
that	**is**	**now**	**quickest**	**to say**

þæt	*ic*	*wilnode*	*weorðfullice*	*to libbanne*
conjunction	pronoun 1st person nominative singular	verb 1st person singular past	adverb	verbal infinitive
that	**I**	**desired**	**worshipfully**	**to live**

þa hwile þe	*ic*	*lifede*	*ond*	*æfter*
adverbial phrase	pronoun 1st person nominative singular	verb 1st person singular past	conjunction	preposition
the while that	**I**	**lived**	**and**	**after**

minum	*life*	*þam*	*mannum*	*to læfanne*
adjective neuter dative singular	noun neuter dative singular	definite article masculine dative plural	noun masculine dative plural	verbal infinitive
my	**life**	**(to) those**	**men**	**to leave**

þe	*æfter*	*me*	*wæren*	*min*
relative pron.	preposition	pronoun 1st person dative singular	verb 3rd plural past subjunctive	adjective neuter accusative singular
who	**after**	**me**	**should be**	**my**

gemynd	*on*	*godum*	*weorcum.*
noun neuter accusative singular	preposition	adjective neuter dative plural	noun neuter dative plural
memory	**in**	**good**	**works.**

"It should now quickly be said that I wished to live piously while I was alive and, after my life, to leave to those people who should come after me my memory in good works."

Vocabulary

The vocabulary of Old English overlaps to a large extent with that of the modern language. Whole passages of modern English can be written in which there are only words which come from Old English, as in the following anonymous comic verse:

> *The man in the wilderness asked of me*
> *How many strawberries grow in the sea?*
> *I answered him as I thought good*
> *As many as red herrings grow in the wood.*

When Neil Armstrong first set foot on the surface of the moon, his famous words "One small step for man, one giant leap for mankind" are almost wholly based on OE vocabulary[3].

However, anyone approaching the language for the first time will be surprised at how little they can read even in a printed edition of a text. This is partly due to the spelling traditions, of course: *cinn* looks as if it should be pronounced 'sin' not 'chin', and *þeof* doesn't look much like 'thief', while *hnutu* (nut) doesn't look as if it is pronounceable at all! Taking the words used by King Alfred in the sentence given in the section above, we may mark those which have survived and those which have fallen by the wayside:

Þæt	*is*	*nu*	*hraþost*	*to secganne*
'that'	'is'	'now'	–	'to say'
ic	*wilnode*	*weorðfullice*	*to libbanne*	*þa hwile þe*
'I'	–	'worthfully'	'to live'	'the while' – while that
lifede	*ond*	*æfter*	*minum*	*life*
'lived'	'and'	'after'	'my'	'life'
þam	*mannum*	*to læfanne*	*þe*	*me*
'the'	'man'	'to leave'	–	'me'
wæren	*gemynd*	*on*	*godum*	*weorcum.*
'were'	'mind'	'on'	'good'	'work'

As you can see from this small sample, some few are no longer in use, such as *wilnode* 'desired' and others have changed their meaning

---

[3] Strictly speaking 'giant' is a Latin-based word, but it has been used in English for well over a thousand years and even occurs in *Beowulf* in the form *gigant* so it may well be regarded as 'naturalized' despite its foreign origins.

somewhat, such as *gemynd* 'remembrance, memory'; *hraþost* 'soonest' has entirely gone but *hraþor* 'sooner' lives on in the word 'rather'.

Unlike the modern language, Old English relied on its own resources for word creation, and only imported 'foreign' words when there were important cultural differences to mark; for example, *sacerd* and *preost* (both words for 'priest' from classical languages) ousted whatever earlier English word existed for the idea, presumably because the native word had pagan overtones. However, the concepts of Christianity were rendered into the vernacular without difficulty, and often with some grace: 'trinity' is called *þrines* 'threeness', 'mercy' is *mildheortnes* 'mild-heart-ness', 'piety' is *arfæstnes* 'honour-fast-ness', and so on. Old English already had the linguistic equipment to encourage making compound words from shorter single words, such as 'determination' – *anmodnes* – 'one-mind-ness' or as we might say, 'single-mindedness'. But it is these compounds that seem so unfamiliar to the beginner, used as he is to seeing anything complicated or new described in Latin-based terminology, until he learns to break them down into their constituents and deduce the meaning. It is fair to say that a native speaker coming to the word 'determination' for the first time would hardly guess its meaning from its components (*de-* 'away' and *termination* 'ending'?) while an Anglo-Saxon would have no such difficulty with *anmodnes*.

Word Studies

A whole area of linguistic science is devoted to the study of particular words, tracing the changes in their meaning through history and how they relate to each other. It is fairly obvious that the modern word 'ship' and the OE *scip* do not denote the same kind of thing even though the pronunciation is virtually identical and the words have a common thread; the historical developments of technology have brought about changes in the material object.

The OE word *dream* is the ancestor of our word 'dream', but 'nocturnal vision' is not its primary meaning; it usually means 'enjoyment, pleasurable experience' as in the poetic compound *seledreamas* 'hall-dreams', the pleasures of life in the warriors' hall, eating, drinking, socializing, receiving gifts and making boastful promises of high deeds to be done. Something of this meaning still attaches to the word ('dreamy' is still used to describe the superlatively glamorous, whether people, cars, holidays, or whatever) but its first association is now with the illusory phenomena experienced during sleep. The OE word for this was *swefn* which has not survived, being ousted by *dream* in mediaeval times.

Taking a slightly more involved example, the OE word *mæl* has a number of meanings including (1) time, occasion; (2) ornament; (3) sign, mark, symbol; (4) cross; (5) sword. Are there five different words here, or are they all different senses of the same word? It is possible to deduce that the meaning 'cross'[4] is a development from the sense 'sign, token' (the sign of the cross) and likewise 'ornament' is a thing decorated with various marks; therefore senses (2), (3) and (4) are seen to be linked. The last meaning, 'sword' is poetic and probably refers to the powerful symbolic quality of the weapon, which is difficult for us to understand now – Anglo-Saxon men swore oaths on their swords as a sign of good faith; nobles handed swords to their retainers as a mark of their faithful service; swords were used in the marriage ceremony, and oaths of loyalty were sworn on the naked blades; the status of free men was displayed by their right to wear the sword; in short, the weapon had a pervasive ritual meaning and importance, and the name *mæl* is probably used of it poetically therefore with the meaning 'symbol, token'. But how does the first meaning fit in? 'Time' is used here in the sense of 'a point in time' which was marked off or counted on some form of tally, therefore this too is a development from the basic sense 'sign'. Interestingly, the word survives into the modern language as 'meal' which originally meant 'fixed time (for eating)' but the notion of 'eating' has now overtaken that of 'time' as the primary sense of the word. *Mæl* is related to another OE word *mal* 'mark' which developed the sense 'spot, blemish', and which gives rise to the modern form 'mole' (in the sense of a dark skin blemish). Would anyone have guessed at a connection between 'meal' and 'mole', I wonder, without knowing the history of the word back to Anglo-Saxon times?

---

[4] Hence Maldon, Essex, is the 'hill of the cross', presumably a local landmark.

Sources of Old English

So, what is written in OE to make it worth the effort of learning? In actual fact, quite a lot of literature of various types has come down to us from Anglo-Saxon times despite the ravages of the Vikings and Normans, the dissolution of the monasteries and the Civil War. I can do no more than scratch the surface here, for obvious reasons. The written material is generally separated into prose and verse, and further subdivided from there, but before going on to look at these two obvious areas I would like to take a short excursion into the less obvious: place-names and personal names.

Place Names

As I mentioned before, the earliest English occurs in place-names in land grants, like the one for Barking Abbey:

> *...terram quae apellatur ricingahaam, budinhaam, deccanhaam, angenlabeshaam, in silva quae dicitur uuidmundesfelt...*

> ... the land which is called *Ricingahaam* (Rainham, Essex?) *Budinhaam* (unidentified)[5], *Deccanhaam* (Dagenham, Essex?), *Angenlabeshaam*[6], in the wood which is called *Uuidmundesfelt*[7] ...

Obviously when specifying English estates there was no practical way of avoiding their names even when they didn't fit very happily into the Latin syntax. Later charters often have a Latin text to which the boundary markers are appended in English, such as this one issued for King Edgar in 962:

---

[5] This territory remains unidentified; however, there is a strong likelihood that either *Budinhaam* or *Angenlabeshaam* (below) is the estate which was later subdivided into East and West Ham (*haam* is an early spelling of the word which gave rise to 'Ham').

[6] *Angenlabeshaam* has never been identified; as it is the 'homestead of (the man called) Angenlaf', when ownership later changed the name may have been altered with it.

[7] *Uuidmundesfelt* is the 'open country of (the man called) Widmund', possibly modern Chadwell Heath, Essex.

These are the land-boundaries for *Mordune* (Mordon, Berkshire): First to the boundary ford (*higford*); from the boundary ford along the reed stream (*hreodburnan*) to the *Worf* stream; along that stream to *Purtanig* westwards; northwards over *Purtanig* back out to *Worf* stream; along the stream to the wooden bridge (*wudebricge*); from there onto the ash-tree pond (*æsclace*) where the ash-tree pond falls out into the *Worf*; up against the stream at the eastern end of the long ploughland (*furlanges*) then east to the old ditch (*ða ealdan dic*); from the old ditch to Grindwyll's pond for one furlong; from there to Ætta's pen (*Ætden pæn*) to the eldertree stump (*ellenstyb*); from there always by the edge to the pastures (*medemunga*); from the pastures downwards to the old willow (*ðone ealdan uuiðig*) on the pond in Atta's pen; from there to the whortleberry ford (*hortan ford*); from the ford to Filica's valley (*filican slæd*); along the valley to the old spring (*ðone ealdan wylle*), from there out to the valley of Headda's hill (*headdandune slæd*); along the valley to the broad way (*bradan weg*), from the broad way along the valley out to the boundary ford.

Many of these boundaries are still traceable today, and the interested student can spend many an absorbing hour with detailed OS maps and Old English charters matching them one against the other. Follow-up work on the ground is often able to resolve areas of uncertainty, since the Anglo-Saxon inhabitants of an area were intimately familiar with its topography and gave names to features which are now sometimes difficult to determine without first-hand observation. That is not to say that one can reasonably expect to come across 'the eldertree stump' or 'the old willow', but one might well find a spot with just the kind of preferred habitat where such a tree might have grown.

In fact, place-names are one of the great refuges of OE vocabulary and place-name studies are one of the few disciplines where it is not simply desirable but essential to have a good knowledge of OE. And it is fair to say that wherever you go in the south and east of England you will be surrounded by an Anglo-Saxon landscape. The great centres of learning (Oxford, Cambridge), of manufacturing industry (Coventry, Birmingham, Wolverhampton) and of recreation (Southend, Bognor, Margate, Brighton) are all named in accordance with Old English practice. Names may be descriptive, such as Slough (*slōh*, muddy place) or Heybridge (*hēah brycg*, a high bridge) or attributive such as Acton (*āc tūn*, oak tree enclosure), or Pinner (*pinn ōra*, peg-shaped slope). Many record the names of presumptive owners, such as Edgware (Æcge's weir), Kenton (*Cēnan tūn*, Cēna's enclosure). A whole group record their one-time settlement by yeomen who owed allegiance directly to the king – these are called in Old English *ceorla tun* 'enclosure of the yeomen', surviving as Charlton, Carlton or Chorlton depending on local dialect. They usually occur next to known royal manors – the king would visit his own estate and call in the rents due from his yeomen, paid in food to be consumed during his stay.

Some of the most interesting examples are not place-names in the strict sense at all, but rather the names of territories, such as Vange, from East Saxon *fæn gē*, (equivalent to West Saxon *fenn-gē*, 'fen district'). Vange is now a small parish on the northern bank of the Thames, but its name was once that of the entire district comprising a marshy region from the Thames to the Rayleigh Hills. East Saxondom was presumably divided into sub-districts, each called a *gē*[8], since the word occurs also in Dengie and Ingatestone, of which the ancient form was *gēinga stān* 'stone of the ge-people'. This brings me to a second type of OE non-place-name, of which there are dozens in the south east: those ending in OE in '-*ingas*'. Interpretation is not easy without very reliable early spellings, but generally it is believed that place-names such as Barking (*Berecingas*), Barling (*Bærlingas*), Havering (*Hæferingas*) are actually the names of social groupings, owing loyalty to named individuals – in these cases *Bearoc, Bærla* and *Hæfer* respectively. These men were probably petty chiefs or local magnates who had come to dominate a sizeable territory (often more than one modern village). It is unfortunately difficult to separate these modern '-ing' names from others, like Clavering (*clæfring*, clover place) which are just descriptive.

Students of place-names are lucky in some respects – a detailed knowledge of the stylistics of prose and verse are totally unnecessary when one is dealing with short, single words made from one or two

---

8 This is the same word as German 'Gau' and is also used in eastern Kent to name its components (e.g. Sturry from *Stur ge*, 'Stour district').

elements. Unfortunately, they cannot afford to skimp on the details of Old English's grammatical background, though. To take an example, a great many place-names are in the 'dative' case, which is to say that they have endings which show location 'at (a place)'. The majority of OE strong nouns form their dative by adding a final -e so that *stan* means 'stone' and *stane* 'at (the) stone'. This is true for masculine nouns (like *stan*), feminine (*stow/stowe* 'place') or neuter (*clif/clife* 'cliff') ones. Weak nouns, take the ending -an whether masculine (*burna/burnan* 'stream') or feminine (*græsmolde/ græsmoldan* 'grassy plain') – and there are no relevant neuters. Therefore the vast majority of datives are covered by the two endings -e and -an. However, there are a few minor patterns of endings which are not covered by these two examples. One is the dative ending in -a which only applies to about a dozen nouns, but three of these are common in place-names: *feld* 'open country', *wudu* 'woodland', *ford* 'ford' (*felda, wuda, forda*). Another is the dative with no actual ending, but with a changed vowel in the middle of the word – again quite a rare type, but the common elements *ac* 'oak tree' and *burg* 'fortress' (dative *æc, byrig*) are among them. This latter case explains the twin forms '-borough' (from *burg*) and '-bury' (from *byrig*) by the way.

Personal Names

Personal names also owe something to the Anglo-Saxons whose name-giving habits were different from our own. For the upper ranks of society at least, the given name was composed of two elements, such as Athelstan, i.e. *æðele stān* 'noble stone'. Some modern individual names are survivals from pre-Conquest times, for example:

Edwin	*ead + wine*	'blessed friend'
Edgar	*ead + gār*	'blessed spear'
Edward	*ead + weard*	'blessed guardian'
Oscar	*ōs + gār*	'god spear'
Randolph	*rand + wulf*	'shield wolf'
Audrey	*æðele + ðryð*	'noble strength'
Gertrude	*gār + ðryð*	'spear strength'

There are, of course, any number of modern names which are of Old English origin but which were not used as names in Anglo-Saxon times – such as Daisy, Lily, Ethel (OE *eðel* 'homeland'), Mitchel (OE *micel* 'great'), Kirk (Old Northumbrian or Norse *kirk* 'church'). There were Anglo-Saxon names not made by compounding, such as *Wulf* 'wolf' and others which were made from a noun or adjective plus a distinctive ending, such as *Golde* (from *gold* 'gold') or *Hwīte* (from *hwīt*, 'white') or *Brāda* (from *brād* 'wide').

Anglo-Saxons also had nicknames which were abbreviated from the fuller forms: *Fobba* from *Folcbeorht*, *Cūða* from *Cūþwine*, and so on. In all likelihood, many modern surnames are survivals from Anglo-Saxon occupational names, such as Hunt (*hunta*, a hunter), Leech (*lǣce*, a doctor), Potter (*pottere*, a potter), Baker and Baxter (*bæcere/bæcestre*, a baker, male/female respectively), Webster (*webbestre*, female weaver). Others, of course, are Old English-based by being transferred from place-names, such as Holt (*holt*, a wood), Higham (*hēah hām*, a high village), Hale (*halh*, a nook). Patronymics could be expressed in two ways: the straightforward Edmondson from *Eadmundes sunu* 'Edmund's son'; or the more ancient method used for example in royal genealogies: *Sigehere Sigeberhting*, where *-ing* shows the relationship (*Sigehere* son of *Sigeberht*).

There is a wealth of linguistic and social history in English personal and place-names, which most of us take for granted like so many other things forming part of our daily lives.

Old English Literature – An Overview

Most literature and records were in Latin at this time, so that England's first great 'historian', *Bædæ* (the Venerable Bede), wrote his scientific and historical works in the tongue of the church. (Record exists of one small scrap of English verse in the story of *Cædmon*, the cowherd who is taught to sing and make poetry by an angel.) This situation would have persisted in England, as it did across most of western Europe, but for the Danish incursions of the ninth century. When all the northern and eastern kingdoms had fallen to piecemeal attacks by the Vikings and only

Wessex stood between them and total victory, the hour brought forth the man, and a very remarkable person came to his country's throne. King Alfred had never expected to rule, being the youngest of several brothers, and had devoted his time to hunting and the study of books. The king won many military victories, but perhaps his greatest and most enduring achievement was in the field of literacy. Realizing how important widespread literacy was to the government and well-being of a strong and prosperous country, Alfred instituted a programme of educational reform centring on vernacular texts. He personally set about translating works of Latin authors into his native tongue so that there should be no lack of properly uplifting and educational material for his people. Very shortly, English versions of standard works began to appear: Orosius's *History against the Pagans*, Bede's *Ecclesiastical History of the English People*, Boethius's *On the Consolation of Philosophy*, Gregory's *Pastoral Care* and just as important as all these, a compilation of annals to form the nucleus of a national record, the so-called *Anglo-Saxon Chronicle*.

This rise in vernacular literature was virtually unique in Europe at this time and was evidently a great success – it brought reading and writing (other than in runes) out of the monastery and into the chief's hall, the merchant's warehouse and the farmer's homestead. The church quickly caught on to the fact that instruction in religious doctrine was both quicker and more complete through use of an English bible, though not all ecclesiastics were entirely happy about translating it. For one thing, the mediaeval attitude to Holy Writ was such that every word and phrase had multiple meanings and even the number of letters in a phrase could have symbolic significance; tampering with this map of creation was at best dangerous and at worst deeply sacrilegious. There were other considerations, too: the English were a fairly robust and independent-minded people, and it was not considered appropriate to introduce them to the fact that the much-respected Abraham had two wives, for example. This was viewed as symbolic or allegorical by the church, but could prove an embarrassing precedent if word got round. Add to that the excesses of bloodshed and fornication in the Old Testament and you had some rather unfortunate role-models for the laity.

The Anglo-Saxon Chronicle

The *Anglo-Saxon Chronicle* was disseminated by copying from a presumed original compilation of records, at six or more religious foundations. Far from being just lists of kings and battles, it contains detailed entries for some years, poems, summaries and personal comment by the annalists. It would be wrong to suggest that much of it is great literature – it wasn't meant to be – but it is a unique record of England in that time and much of it is interesting reading. Like many great works, it leaves you wanting more, but there are no directly comparable works in OE from this time.

Many towns and villages are first recorded in the Chronicle, which concentrates on the south and southwest in its earlier records, spreading its net wider with the reconquest of the Midlands from the Danes in the tenth century. Here are a couple of typical entries – one early, the other from later in the period:

> 790. In this year Archbishop Ianbriht died; and the same year Abbot Æðelheard was chosen as archbishop; and Osred king of the Northumbrians was betrayed and driven from the kingdom; and Æðelred son of Æðelwald received the kingdom again.

> 914. In this year the Viking army rode out over Easter from Northampton and Leicester; and they broke the peace treaty and slew many men at Hokenorton and thereabouts; and very soon after that, as the others were returning, they formed another troop which rode out against Leighton (Buzzard); and then the people of the land were aware of them; and they fought against them and put them to total flight and rescued all that they had seized, as well as a large portion of their horses and weapons.

Other Historical Documents

The Chronicle was not the only document with historical interest, however. A great many other writings serve to build up a picture of life in Anglo-Saxon times. One such is the text called *Sermo Lupi ad Anglos*

(Wolf's Sermon to the English) which was delivered by Wulfstan, bishop of Worcester (later Archbishop of York) in 1014. It gives a moving picture of a society beginning to disintegrate under the pressure of constant Viking assaults:

...But it is true, what I say, the remedy (for a list of troubles) is needed; for God's dues have diminished too long in this nation on every side, and traditional laws have grown far too much worse; and sanctuaries are too widely bereft of peace; and God's houses are too cleanly deprived of ancient dues and stripped from inside of all suitable ornaments; and widows are forced wrongfully to marry men, and too many of them impoverished and greatly shamed; and poor people are painfully deceived and cruelly tricked, and sold out of this country into the power of foreigners; and widely through this nation small children are sent into penal slavery through cruel, unjust laws for a small theft; and the rights of the free taken away, and the rights of thralls reduced, and the duty of almsgiving diminished; and most quickly to be said, God's laws have become hateful and teachings become despised; and from this we all have continual insult through God's anger, let him acknowledge this who knows it; and the injury will become common to all this nation, even though one may hope otherwise, unless God protect us...

It is easy to overplay the apocalyptic vision of Wulfstan and others, who we should recall had a heavy vested interest in the maintenance of the *status quo*, especially where church dues were concerned. When England finally got its first Danish monarchs – Sweyn Forkbeard and his son, Cnut (Canute) – they saw fit to disturb very little of the existing social systems, so it can hardly have been as totally dismal as Wulfstan's writings suggest.

Another cleric, Ælfric the Homilist, compiled a series of worthy and uplifting works on a variety of subjects with a theme of saints' days, but some set in England and recording local tradition (Ælfric probably got his information from Bede's works). Though they are meant to be read as hagiography, they often contain small snippets of interest, such as this from the *Life of King Oswald*:

That same cross which Oswald raised there in honour stood there...
That place is called *Heofenfeld* (Heavenfield) in English, by the long
wall which the Romans wrought, where Oswald overcame that
vicious king (Cadwalla of Wessex). And there a very famous church
was built, to the honour of God, which remains for ever in eternity.

A church on that spot by Hadrian's Wall still exists to this day, called St.
Oswald's, next to a plot called 'Heavenfield'.

Another cleric, also called Ælfric, wrote an intriguing work to assist
in the teaching of Latin to English schoolchildren – *The Colloquy on the
Occupations*. It features a main text in Latin with interlinear glosses
(translations into the vernacular, written in tiny, cramped letters between
the lines of the Latin wording) which can be used in reverse for us to
understand the Old English better. Here is one of the perennial favourites
of schoolmasters teaching foreign languages, the 'imagined
conversation' – this time between a 'magister' and a merchant
concerning his usefulness to the community:

"What do you say, merchant?"

"I say that I am of service to the king, and to the chiefs, and to the
wealthy, and to all people."

"And how so?"

"I go up in my ship with my cargoes, and row across the regions of
the sea, and I sell my goods, and I buy some valuable thing which
is not produced in this land, and I load it back here with great risk
over the sea, and sometimes I undergo shipwreck with the loss of
all my goods, escaping alive only with difficulty."

"Which things do you load for us?"

"Fine robes and silks, valuable gems and gold, rare garments and
mixed spices, wine and oil, ivory and brass, bronze and tin,
sulphur and glass and various other things."

"Will you sell your things here at the same price as you bought them
there?"

"I will not. What use to me would my effort then be? Rather I will
sell them here dearer than I buy them there so that I may acquire
some profit from which I feed myself, and my wife and my sons."

Such little vignettes of daily life are scarce in the early mediaeval literature of Europe, and the whole of the *Colloquy* is a fascinating glimpse into the life of those times, no matter that the conversations are more than a little contrived to demonstrate points of Latin grammar and syntax.

Translations and Other Sources

As mentioned previously, the educational reforms under Alfred caused a demand for uplifting and interesting material in Old English. Partly this was met by the traditional means of the language – story-telling and so on – and the hunger for knowledge of the wide world, both past and present, led to the collection of some varied material. Most of this was translated from Latin, since Greek was not generally read at this time.

There was, in early mediaeval times, a fascination with the military achievements and journeyings of Alexander the Great, which was part of a long classical literary tradition. One view of Alexander saw him as a megalomaniac whose excessive pride drove him ever on to new conquests; another treated him more sympathetically as an explorer whose quest for new marvels led him to seek out the strange and unusual wherever it might be found. The Anglo-Saxon tradition leant more to the latter view, and a translation of a Latin text *The Letter of Alexander to Aristotle* was included in the same manuscript as *Beowulf* (see below), of which the following is a fairly typical scene:

Then the land was all dried out as we travelled, and fens and canes and reeds grew. Then suddenly there came from the fen and refuge a certain animal, and its back was all ridged like a snood, and its head was rounded like the moon, and the beast was called 'quasi caput luna' ("head like the moon") and its chest was like a sea-monster's breast, and with hard teeth, and it was well-armed and toothed. And the animal slew two of my thanes; nor could we wound the beast neither with a spear nor with any weapon, but with difficulty we felled it with iron hammers and mallets, and beat it to death.

This account may be based on an encounter with a crocodile.

Biblical translations were seemingly popular, as well as other classical works with a strong educational theme. Alfred himself is credited with the translation of some of these works. The Greek stories of Ulysses and Circe and of Orpheus and Eurydice were turned into measured Old English prose, to which the king appended his own thoughts on the nature of government:

Lo, you know that no man can display any skill, nor tell nor direct any power without tools and materials. The material of any craft is that without which one cannot go about that craft. Therefore a king's material and tools with which to rule shall be that he have his kingdom properly manned – he must have praying men and fighting men and working men. Lo, you know that without these tools no king can display his skill. It is also his material, that he shall have the necessities for these tools, for these three groups of men. Therefore these are their necessities: land on which to live, and gifts, and weapons, and food, and ale, and clothes, and whatever else is proper for these three groups. Without these things he cannot wield these tools, nor without these tools carry out any of those things which he is required to carry out.

Alfred's court was a centre for traders and visitors from far and wide, and at the height of his wars with the Danes he still found time and opportunity to enquire of a Norwegian merchant about the nature of his homeland. The Norseman, Ohthere by name, described in some detail to the king the way of life of his people and related the story of a trip he had made to the land of the Lapps; Alfred's curiosity about foreign lands and peoples must have been truly whetted by this. Concerning his own country, Ohthere said:

...that the land of the Northmen was very long and very narrow. All of it which can be grazed or ploughed lies next to the sea, and that is very rocky in places; and wild moorlands lie eastwards and upwards alongside the inhabited land. On those moorlands dwell the Lapps. And the inhabited land is widest to the east, and becomes narrower the further north. In the east it may be sixty miles wide or a little wider, and in the middle thirty or more, and to the north where it is narrowest, he said that it might be three miles wide over to the moorland; and the moorland afterwards in some places so wide that one could cross it in two weeks, and in other places so wide that one could cross it in six days.

Law-Codes

Alfred took the trouble to re-issue an old law-code with his own amendments rather than create one *de novo*. Being founded in existing tradition, his laws had higher status than some other OE codes may have had. Many of the 'Laws' are no more than listings of fines payable by various grades of freemen in given circumstances. They offer small vignettes of early English life, for example:

Be stale (concerning theft).

If any should steal so that his wife does not know, nor his children, let him pay 60 shillings as a fine. If he should steal with the knowledge of all his family, let them all go into slavery. A ten-year-old boy may be considered an accomplice to theft.

Be wuda bærnette (in the matter of burning a wood)

When someone burns down a tree in a wood and it becomes known as to who did it, let him pay the full fine: he shall give 60 shillings, because fire is a thief.

If someone should fell a good many trees in a wood, and should afterwards be discovered, let him pay for three trees, each at 30 shillings. Nor need he pay for more, no matter how many there may have been, because the axe is an informant not a thief.

You may care to reflect on the principles behind these two cases. In the first, someone who sneaks away with goods and hides them bears sole responsibility, but if stolen goods are found where the family must have been aware of them, then they are communally guilty and lose their free status as a punishment – the incentive to turn in the miscreant must have been great with so much at stake for the whole family.

In the second example, the man who sets fire to a tree has deprived its owner of it and has to recompense him; but a man who fells a load of timber in a wood would make a lot of noise and the onus would then be on the landowner to come and intervene. Hence the cryptic remark that "an axe is an informant, not a thief".

There are several Anglo-Saxon law-codes in existence, and they become fuller and more expansive with time. The code of the Danish king Cnut – better known to us as Canute – is probably the most encyclopaedic, though all these documents are really designed to set fines and compensation rather than to establish legal and illegal behaviour in the modern sense.

Family Documents

More personal documents also exist: wills and gifts and grants of land; some were still in Latin, especially where the church was involved, but many were written in English. They tend to follow a set formula: "This is the will of X, how his/her possessions are to be divided after his/her day... " and so on. This is the will of the lady Æþelflæd, the second wife of King Edmund, whose sister Ælfflæd was married to Ealdorman Byrhtnoð, the hero of the poem *The Battle of Maldon*.

> This is Æþelflæd's will. That is first that I grant to my lord the land at *Lamburnan* (Lambourn, Berks.) and that at *Ceolsige* (Cholsey, Berks.) and at *Readingan* (Reading, Berks.); and four rings of two hundred mancuses (a unit of weight) of gold, and four robes, and four cups, and four dishes, and four horses. And I bid my dear lord for the love of God that my will may stand. And I have made no other in God's witness. And I grant that land at *Domarhame* (Damerham, Wilts.) to Glastonbury for the soul of King Edmund, and that of King Edgar and of my own. And I grant that land at *Hamme* (unidentified) to Christ's church at Canterbury for the soul of King Edmund, and for my soul. And I grant that land at *Wudaham* (Woodham, Essex) to Ealdorman Byrhtnoð and to my sister for her day, and after her day to St. Mary's church at Barking. And I grant that land at *Hedham* (Hadham, Herts.) to Ealdorman Byrhtnoð and to my sister for her day,

and after her day to St. Paul's borough in London as an episcopal estate. And I grant the land at *Dictunæ* (Fen Ditton, Cambs.) to Ely, to St. Æþelðryð and her group of sisters. And I grant the two lands at *Cohhanfeldæa* (Cockfield, Suffolk) and at *Cæorlesweorþe* (Chelsworth, Suffolk) to Ealdormann Byrhtnoð and my sister for her day, and after her day to St. Edmund's foundation at *Bydericeswyrðe* (Bury St. Edmunds – the older name 'Bedricksworth' has now been supplanted by the religious one). And I grant that land at *Fingringaho* (Fingringhoe, Essex) to Ealdorman Byrhtnoð and my sister for her day, and after her day to St. Peter's church at Mersea. And I grant that land at *Polstede* (Polstead, Suffolk) to Ealdorman Byrhtnoð and my sister for her day, and after her day to Stoke-by-Nayland. And I grant that land at *Hwifermersce* (Withermarsh, Suffolk) to Stoke-by-Nayland after my day. And I grant to Ealdorman Byrhtnoð and my sister the land at *Strætforda* (Stratford St. Mary, Suffolk) for her day and after her day I grant it to Stoke-by-Nayland. And I wish that *Lauanham* (Lavenham, Suffolk) shall go to Stoke-by-Nayland after the ealdorman's day and my sister's. And I grant that land at *Byligesdynæ* (Balsdon hall, Suffolk) to Stoke-by-Nayland after the ealdorman's day and my sister's. And I grant the lands at *Peltandune* (Peldon, Essex) and at *Myresige* (Mersea, Essex) and at *Grenstede* (Greenstead, Essex) after my day, and after Ealdorman Byrhtnoð's and after my sister's. And I grant that land at *Ylmesæton* (Elmsett, Suffolk) to Ealdorman Byrhtnoð and to my sister for her day, and after her day I grant it to Edmund. And I grant the one hide (a unit of land) at *Þorpæ* (Thorpe Morieux, Suffolk) to Hadleigh for my soul and for those of my ancestors, after my day.

Some of these documents record how the testator came by the land or property, establishing and reinforcing the entitlement of subsequent holders. One such text, dated 961, concerns a Kentish lady called Eadgifu:

Eadgifu declares to the archbishop and the community of Christ's church how the land at Cooling came to her, which is that her father left her land and charter, as he rightfully obtained them, and as his ancestors bequeathed it to him. It happened that her father borrowed 30 pounds from Goda, and entrusted him with the land as security for the money, and he held it for 7 years. Then it came about at that time that all the Kentish folk were summoned to war, to Holm. Sigelm, her father, did not wish to ride to war with any man's money unrepaid, and so he gave back the 30 pounds to Goda and made over the land to Eadgifu, his daughter, and gave her written entitlement. When he had been cut down in battle, Goda denied the repayment of the money and withheld the land.

The story goes on at some length, about how Eadgifu took the matter to the local court and from there the king became involved, but with the early deaths of many tenth century English monarchs no satisfactory solution was ever found and enforced before the process had to start all over again. Edweard, Æðelstan, and Eadred all sat in judgement, but it fell to Eadgar to finally resolve the conflict in favour of the lady, who eventually made the land over to the church in gratitude.

Family disputes such as this must have been common and it is somehow reassuring to find the familiar motives of our day reflected in the past: repayment of debt, greedy exploitation of the apparently defenceless, steadfast opposition to injustice, and inexhaustible patience in going through the whole case before four successive kings.

Medical and Magical Texts

Another group of texts which call forth an immediate response are the so-called *Leechdoms*, medical and medicinal treatises. There are several of these; some direct translations of Graeco-Latin originals, others betraying their probable northern European origins. The OE *Herbarium* is a Latin-based collection, listing herbs and their uses, for example: Number 89 *herba erusti* which is the blackberry (1) against soreness of the ears, (2) against a woman's bloodflow, (3) against heart pain, (4) against recent wounds, (5) against soreness of the limbs and (6) against snakebite.

The remedy itself just says, in the case of snakebite:

> "Against an adder's bite take this same plant's leaf which we call *erusti* newly pounded, and lay it on the wound."

41

Not all the remedies are as straightforward as this, however, since showmanship has always been part of the process of effecting a cure. Take a treatment for sore eyes:

"Eyesalve. Take a strawberry, the lower part, and a pepper – put it in a cloth and bind it on – put on sweetened wine, dripping from the cloth, one drop in each eye – if the eyes be obstructed, take raven's gall and a white mastic, lettuce and salmon's gall, put them all together and drip them into the eye through a flax-coloured cloth as a slightly acidic juice – then the eye will waken."

These medical books are supplemented by other remedies, what we would call charms or spells or rituals. There is some argument as to what these texts are really about, some scholars seeing them as debased mimicry of church ritual, others as survivals of pre-Christian belief. References to God, Mary and various saints are common in the charms, although often these are vague and have only a tenuous link with accepted Christian doctrine.

For Stolen Cattle. This must a man say when someone has stolen one of his cattle, let him say it before he may say any other word "Bethlehem is the name of the town where Christ was born, it is renowned over all Middle-earth; so may this deed be known among men. PER CRUCEM CRISTI" and pray thrice to the east and say thrice "CRUX CRISTI AB ORIENTE REDUCAT" and then west and say "CRUX CRISTI AB OCCIDENTE REDUCAT" and then south and say thrice "CRUX CRISTI AMERIDIE REDUCAT" and then north and say "CRUX CRISTI ABSCONDITA ET INVENTA EST. The Jews hanged Christ, they did to him the worst of deeds: they covered up what they could not hide away – so may this deed never be hidden away. PER CRUCEM CRISTI."

While this looks like an optimistic attempt to invoke divine assistance in tracking down a cattle-rustler, there are other charms which seem definitely older, belonging to a world where the movements of animals could be used to divine the future – or rather, since the future in our sense did not figure in the English world view, to discern the pattern of events as they unfold.

Wiþ Ymbe (**In Case of a Bee Swarm**) Take some earth, throw it with your right hand under your right foot and say "I take it from under the foot, I have found what earth can do against all kinds of things, against hatred and against forgetfulness and against the mighty tongue of man." And then throw grit over them as they swarm and say "Sit, women of victory, sink to earth, never fly wild to the wood, but be as mindful of my welfare as any man may be of his food and homeland."

The 'women of victory' image has been likened to the idea of the Valkyries, powerful female warlike spirits who are equally at home on earth or in the air and who can bestow blessings or curses on human beings. It may be that this bee-charm is of very ancient date and an almost unique survival of pre-Christian lore coming down without any obvious Christian influence.

Poems

This charm, like many others, is formally not prose but a song or poem. We know from the account of Tacitus, the Roman writer of the 1st century AD who described the customs and life of the Germanic peoples, that their records and stories took the form of songs, and indeed OE verse is as highly wrought as the early prose is plain. Clearly, the OE singer or poet was also the storyteller, and the tales of long ago, of gods and elves and heroes, were all delivered in the complicated sacred and ritual language we call verse. It is no accident that prose texts, such as the early annals in the Chronicle, tend to be curt and repetitive – slightly later entries are more ambitious but the result is usually a series of short statements linked by 'and' and 'but' and 'then'. Handling lengthy prose descriptions of events factually clearly did not come easy to the writers of these annals, and the shortcomings of early English prose are hard to understand – easy to deride – unless we bear in mind the fact that battles and accessions and the deaths of kings had hitherto been expressed formally in the ritual language of verse. It probably took a great deal of restraint not to begin annals with *Hwæt! We gefrunon...* (a traditional kind of opening for momentous verse)

To put this in a slightly different context, we may say that the oldest English writings are the rune texts and the charter place-names, but the most archaic is certainly the verse. Sadly for us, the singer's performance was always extemporized and unique, so that no OE poem can be said to have existed in its recorded form exactly until the poet came to write or dictate it himself. Before that the verse framework was rigid while the form was fluid; writing fixed the form. In other words, every telling was a unique performance, a single event, and the poet had complete freedom to put emphasis on different aspects of the tale according to the occasion or his audience's mood. He could also introduce other elements as necessary, parallel stories or contrasting ones, recent events or ancient legends – all these matters could occupy either a half-dozen lines or a hundred according to his wishes. The verse medium was flexible enough to accommodate anything the poet wished to do with it. But poets have to earn a living and the patronage of great men rests in large part in pleasing and entertaining them. This could mean praising their warlike valour and noble ancestry, or if they were clergymen it meant narrating biblical stories in verse.

Verse Metre

The metre of Old English was not at all similar to what we might think of as verse. For one thing, there was no fixed pattern of 'beats in a bar' producing the 'tum-ti-tum' effect, and for another there was no rhyme (or, more accurately, rhyme was not a feature of the verse – although it was sometimes used to decorate Old English poetry). How, then, did it work?

Conventionally, OE verse worked at two levels – the 'line' and the 'half-line'. Each line consisted of two half-lines, each of two stressed syllables and a number of unstressed ones. The stressed syllables are the ones that are naturally longer and rhythmically louder in speech. Taking an example from modern English (the stressed syllables are underlined, and '/' marks the break between the half-lines):

Winston Churchill / wrote a letter

If you pronounce this phrase with normal intonation, you will see how the 'stressed' syllables are louder and spoken with more force than the other, unstressed ones. Because Old English words are generally stressed on their first syllable, the pattern shown above is quite common in the corpus of poetry. Another common pattern is:

a cup of tea / and a piece of cake

where the stressed syllables now follow the unstressed ones. A mixture of these and other rhythmic types is possible. If we mark a stressed syllable as 'S', a partly-stressed one as 's' and an unstressed one (or more than one) as 'x' we can draw up the following summary of the five basic types of half-line:

Type	Pattern	Example
A	SxSx	Winston Churchill
B	xSxS	a piece of cake
C	xSSx	a small fortune
D	SSsx	sleep fitfully
E	SsxS	buying a house

In Old English usage, the stressed syllables had to be 'heavy', which is to say that they had to have a long vowel (*stān*) or end in two consonants (*word*); the poets could cheat and use a word with two light syllables (*werod*). Taking the word *stān* as an example, when its various endings are added (*stānes, stāne, stānas, stāna, stānum*) these forms automatically produce the metrical pattern 'Sx', making it easy to build half-lines (types A, B and C all use this pattern) from it, e.g. *stānes āgend* 'a stone's owner' (type A) or *oð stāna clif* 'up to the stones' cliff' (Type B).

A further refinement in the technique is alliteration. In principle, two or three of the four stressed syllables should alliterate (begin with the same sound); the third stressed syllable must always carry alliteration while the fourth should not. Therefore the possible patterns are (remember we are only dealing with the four stressed syllables in a full line now):

AB / AC　　　　**BA / AC**　　　　**AA / AC**

Sometimes the pattern of alliteration can be slightly more decorative. It may be doubled up into two sets of separately alliterating syllables, when it is either crossed: AB / AB or transverse: AB / BA. Crossed alliteration obviously violates the principle that the final syllable should not alliterate.

For poetic purposes, all vowels are considered to alliterate together (or perhaps we should say that syllables beginning with a vowel alliterate on a 'zero' consonant). The treatment of initial 's-' varies, and, in what may represent the purest tradition, where a cluster of consonants beginning with 's-' starts a stressed syllable, it is ignored – so that *stēam* can alliterate with *stān* and *sling* with *slidor* but not with each other; certainly, *sc-* never goes with anything but *sc-*.

To give a short example of the metre in action, here are two lines from the tenth century poem *The Battle of Maldon*:

Þa þæt <u>Of</u>fan <u>m</u>æg	<u>æ</u>rest on<u>fu</u>nde
Then that Offa's kinsman	first found out
þæt se <u>eorl</u> <u>n</u>olde	<u>y</u>rhðo ge<u>b</u>olian
that the earl would not	slackness
	tolerate

The metrical patterns are therefore:

xxSxS (Type B)	SxxSx (Type A)
xxSSx (Type C)	SxxSx (Type A)

and the alliterative one is AB / AC in both cases – alliterating on the vowels of *Offan, ærest* and *eorl, yrhðo*.

Verse Riddles

There was a long tradition of word-play in the north, perhaps not always in verse but the most notable surviving examples are the riddles, some of which appear to be home-grown while others are translations of Latin *Enigmata*. Many collections must once have existed, but virtually the only surviving examples come from one manuscript, the Exeter Book.

Here is a short one:

A moth ate words	– to me that seemed
a remarkable event	when I learnt of the marvel
that the insect gulped down	part of a man's speech
– the thief in the dark	– his glorious saying
and its strong foundation.	The thieving visitor was not
a whit the wiser	for having digested those words.

The answer is of course a bookworm, munching his way through the vellum of a book.

Beowulf

There is no space here to look in any detail at the many fine poems which have come down to us in Old English. But we could hardly pass by OE verse without looking at the only surviving masterpiece of its age – probably the only piece of pre-Chaucerian writing of which most people have heard: *Beowulf*. I actually began my OE studies with a copy of *Beowulf* and a grammar, which is almost certainly the worst possible introduction – the poem is very long, quite complex and features lots of strange, poetic words and convoluted syntactic patterns. But after *Beowulf*, everything else is like coasting with the wind at your back!

Let me remind you of the story of the young hero, Beowulf, who hears of a monster terrorizing the Danish king's hall and resolves to fight it. In a nocturnal wrestling match Grendel, the monster, realizes he has met his match and flees, leaving his arm and hand in our hero's titanic grip. General rejoicing and quaffing of mead follows, as well as some major gift-giving by the king, but joy turns to sorrow when next night sees Grendel's mother mount a vengeance raid which carries off one of the king's best men. Beowulf tracks the hag down to her underwater lair and hews off her head with a giant's sword; back at the royal hall, the king hands over more treasure and counsels the young victor in statesmanship. Beowulf returns to his people, the Geats, rises to a position of honour and, with the death of the rightful heir, takes the throne. His people's enemies are unwilling to test their military strength against the Geats, and all passes quietly until a dragon begins ravaging the land. The king and his war band plan to surprise the beast in its lair, but the warriors are not accustomed to earning their keep and choose to desert their leader when he needs them most. One youngster stands by him, though, and together they slay the firedrake, but at the cost of the king's life. The retainer predicts woe for his people now their protector is dead and the poem ends with the raising of the burial mound which is to be his only monument.

The tone of the original is virtually impossible to convey succinctly in our modern tongue, but the following is offered as a taste of the verse with no claims to have reproduced the terse majesty of the Old English. King Hroþgar counsels the young Beowulf about the dangers of pride which may attend great achievements such as his, reminding him of the inevitable processes of change in the world:

> Ward off dire hatred from yourself, dear Beowulf,
> best of men, and choose what is best for you,
> everlasting good counsels; do not incline to pride,
> renowned champion. Now the fame of your skill is
> for a short time only; it shall soon be
> that sickness or sword deprives you of your strength,
> or fire's grip, or water's surge,
> or sword's bite, or spear's flight,
> or deadly old age; or your eyes' brightness
> fails and grows dim; it must ever be
> that death shall overcome you, noble warrior.

> *Bebeorh þe ðone bealonið Beowulf leofa*
> *secga betsta ond þe þæt selre geceos*
> *ece rædas oferhyda ne gym*
> *mære cempa. Nu is þines mægnes blæd*
> *ane hwile eft sona bið*
> *þæt þec adl oððe ecg eafoþes getwæfeð*
> *oððe fyres feng oððe flodes wylm*
> *oððe gripe meces oððe eagena bearhtm*
> *forsiteð ond forsworceð semninga bið*
> *þæt ðec dryhtguma dead oferswyðeð.*

(*Beowulf* lines 1758 – 68)

This poem is over 3,000 lines long and contains more flashbacks, digressions, timeshifts, and story-within-a-story episodes than any poet has the right to indulge in, yet it is probably the only 'popular' early English poem today. Its plot is not balanced, nor is the point of all the incidental material clear, yet most readers feel that it holds together remarkably well and there are clear themes and ideas the poet is trying to put across. Modern critics have analysed the text ad infinitum, and there are some very readable modern versions in prose and verse, but nothing compares with sitting down armed with pen and paper and working your way through it, reading the poem in the original in its own verse style and in the words of the anonymous Anglo-Saxon poet who first committed it to writing.

The Exeter Book

Our knowledge of Old English verse in general and in detail would be immeasurably poorer without one single volume, the so-called Exeter Book which was given to the cathedral of Exeter by Bishop Leofric in the early years of the eleventh century and has been there ever since. It is the only known complete volume of early English verse which could not have been put together by a later collector of mediaeval manuscripts – it is in fact a true Anglo-Saxon selection of material, and fairly eclectic it is too.

As befits a bishop's gift to his cathedral, the book contains many religious poems on biblical themes, such as *Christ*, *The Descent into Hell*, *Judgement Day*, *Pharaoh*, and the *Lord's Prayer*. It also has some Christian-allegorical material such as *The Phoenix* (a symbol of Christ reborn), *Juliana* (the mother of the first Christian Roman emperor, who was believed to have retrieved the True Cross) and *Azarias*. Invocations to Christian living and warnings against worldliness are included (*Vainglory*, *Precepts*, *The Gifts of Men*, *Resignation*, *Alms-Giving*, *Homiletic Fragment*), and a verse story of St. Guthlac, an Anglo-Saxon warrior who retreated into the Fens to do spiritual battle with demons. What is difficult to explain is the other material in the book, some of which is very puzzling. Two poems, *The Wanderer* and *The Seafarer*, deal with the hardships of life in the world and may be read as allegorical commentaries. The first of them begins in mournful mood like this:

> A solitary man often   waits for mercy,
> the mildness of *Metod* (God)   though with sorrowing mind he
> – over the waterway –   for a long time had to
> stir with his hands   the ice-sold sea,
> walk the exile-ways   – the course of events is fixed.

Many of the sixty or so *Riddles* have precious little to do with the Church or Christianity – some few are very lewd! *Widsith* tells the story of an imagined journey by an early poet across most of Germanic Europe, meeting the famed kings and heroes of the great tribes on the way. Even with the (fairly clumsy) addition of biblical figures, this poem must rank among the earliest in any Germanic language. Likewise, *Deor* is a short, stanzaic exploration of stoic endurance in the face of life's uncertainties; it is unique in Old English verse in having a repeated 'chorus'. To illustrate, one verse runs:

> To Beadulhild was not   the death of her brothers
> so painful in her heart   as her own affair,
> that she readily   had understood
> that she was pregnant   – she could never
> reflect with courage   how it might be about that.
> That passed away   so may this.

The lady's fears were unfounded for, although she had been raped by her brothers' slayer, the child turned out to be one of the greatest heroes of Germanic tradition.

If these poems were not unlikely enough material, the book also includes *Wulf and Eadwacer*, a short poem apparently telling of the longing of a woman for her outlawed lover, who she expects will take their son off with him to the woods. The *Maxims* are a collection of statements about how things are in the world and what is their proper function. *The Wife's Lament* explores the feelings of a noblewoman whose husband has been forced to flee into exile, and who now endures a miserable life awaiting his call to join him. One cannot help but be touched by the doleful sentiments so movingly expressed in these first few lines:

I craft this song	about myself so sorrowfully,
my own experience.	That I can tell –
what I have undergone of woes	since I grew up,
– both old and new,	never greater than now.
I have always won hardship	through my journeys in exile.

The Husband's Message, strangely, records a message by a husband to his wife to come and join him overseas where he has made his fortune. *The Ruin* is a trip through a ruined town, reflecting on the transience of human life and the deceptive nature of all that men put their trust in.

As poems go, there is no obvious link between these many different examples. Some are very long (e.g. *Widsith*), others very short (e.g. *Deor*); some are obviously Christian (e.g. *The Lord's Prayer*), but many barely so (e.g. *Maxims, Widsith*); some have a clear theme (*Guthlac*), others seem to have little point at all (*Wulf and Eadwacer*). What was in the mind of Bishop Leofric when he had the collection made is hard to guess, and the book may have been nothing more than a convenient manual for him to use in recording striking poems, of whatever sort, which he wanted to be able to read. Frankly, the whole collection is quite puzzling to modern scholars, some of whom have tried to find biblical or Patristic motifs in all the various poems, although the reasoning used for this can be very tenuous at times.

Why Learn Old English ?

This brings me back to the second question I raised earlier: why learn Old English? It is, after all, a dead language and quite a lot of the writings available in it can also be found in Latin. But this misses the point: the essence of our early language and culture is in the home-grown material – the Chronicle and the laws, the charms, the riddles and Beowulf. These works are surviving examples of a once-large corpus and only historical accident has allowed these few scraps to be handed down over the thousand years which separate us from their composers. Old English is both old and English and we ought to value it for being both these things. We have probably the largest and certainly the most varied and interesting literature from early mediaeval Europe, and it can all be read by anyone today, mostly in edited texts available in cheap paperback editions costing less than a round of drinks or a cinema ticket. You and I are heirs to this long tradition, this cultural continuum, by virtue of being speakers of the English language preserved for us by Alfred of Wessex, and never since silenced even when the literature was suppressed under the Normans. We can read the words of Alfred, composing poetry or addressing his bishops; or of Wulfstan haranguing his countrymen for their ungodly ways. If you have the patience, you can stand in the British Library in front of a glass case and read about Scyld Scefing's funeral in the one-and-only original *Beowulf* manuscript, which is on permanent display.

Old English — New English

And one final thought before I close: to anyone who is unaware of its roots, the modern language will always seem haphazard and arbitrary. The student of OE cannot help but look with fresh eyes at English and see connections he would never have guessed at before. He learns, for example, about a set of vowel correspondences between parts of the same word – the very ones which produce pairs such as 'man/men' and 'foot/feet' and he can very soon apply this knowledge to a host of other pairs which he would hardly have guessed at otherwise:

doom (judgement)	with	deem (to judge)
room	with	ream (make room)
rise (go up)	with	rear (bring up)
lose	with	(for)lorn
cold	with	chill
knot	with	knit
full	with	fill

day	with	dawn (become day)
sew (join)	with	seam (a joint)
moon	with	month
stirrup	with	stye (thing for climbing) rope

The path from Old English to the modern language can be traced for many words, allowing us to see the developments in sound and establish correspondences between the two languages. Generally speaking, the consonantal skeletons of the words are constant, while the vowels may undergo various changes. Modern spelling and other factors often obscure the neat pattern, however:

OE	NE	OE examples	NE examples
a	a	*daroð, gatu*	dart, gates
ā	oa / o-e	*stān, bān, āc, bāt*	stone, bone, oak, boat
æ	a	*cæt, bæþ*	cat, bath
ǣ	ea, ee	*rǣd, dǣd, spǣc*	read, deed, speech
e	e	*ecg, cwencan*	edge, quench
ē	ee, ea	*mētan, dēman, wērig*	meet, deem, weary
i	i	*gif, lifer*	if, liver
ī	i-e	*hwīl, gelīc*	while, alike
o	o	*god, bodig, longung*	god, body, longing
ō	oo	*bōna, mōd, flōd*	boon, mood, flood
u	u	*bucca, lust*	buck, lust
ū	ou, ow	*mūs, nū, cū*	mouse, now, cow
y	i	*synn, hyll, cyssan*	sin, hill, kiss
ȳ	i-e	*rȳfe, hlȳstan*	rife, listen

(**Note:** the modern words have evolved from the OE ones and so do not always have the same meaning.)

The correspondences set out above are no more than a summary and do not take account of the long history of individual words. To take an example, the OE word *rād* meant, amongst other things, 'the act of riding; a journey; a place where one rides'. From this third sense it developed into the modern word 'road' (place for riding). However, in northern dialects ā becomes 'ai' and therefore *rād* became 'raid' with the first and second senses, which later became especially associated with a journey on military service or for aggressive purposes. The two modern words 'road' and 'raid' have developed from a single OE original.

This northern change from 'ā' to 'ai' accounts for Scots dialect 'stain' (stone), 'laird' (lord), etc.

I have only been able to give you a sample of what OE studies are about, but I hope you will agree with me that it is a broad and interesting subject which repays the careful study it deserves, but nonetheless has a great deal to offer those whose interest is only loosely connected, be they historians, linguists, English students, archaeologists, sociologists, or whatever. All of you who have read and understood this short summary are heirs of the Anglo-Saxons by virtue of using their language. The least we can do in fairness to those folk is to let them speak for themselves.

Where do I go from here?

Below are some suggestions for further reading. There are a great many books on the history of English literature which begin in the (linguistic) modern period with Shakespeare and his immediate predecessors; others take Chaucer as their starting point, although the mental dexterity and sheer effort required to read Chaucer in the original is at least as great as that needed to read Alfred.

All these titles should be currently available in (or through) bookshops. They are all suitable for the interested reader with little or no specialist knowledge, many having been written specifically as introductions to their subjects.

I. General Introductions

(a) The Anglo-Saxon Period

Keynes, S. and Lapidge, M. *Alfred the Great* Penguin 1983
Comprehensive and illuminating introduction to the sources of our knowledge of this most famous of Anglo-Saxon period kings; contains a full translation of Asser's *Life of King Alfred,* relevant entries from the *Anglo-Saxon Chronicle*, and other works attributed to Alfred himself. Part of the "Penguin Classics" series.

Myres, J. N. L. *The English Settlements* Oxford University Press, 1986
Part of the "Oxford History of England" dealing with the settlement period, relying mainly on archaeological evidence.

Richards, J. D. *The English Heritage Book of Viking Age England* Batsford, 1991
Companion volume to Welch's (below) dealing with the middle to late Saxon periods.

Sherley-Price, L. Bede : *A History of the English Church and People* Penguin, 1955
Indispensable source document for the earlier period of Anglo-Saxon history and the early church; a "Penguin Classic".

Stenton, F. M. *Anglo-Saxon England* Oxford University Press, 1971
The classic reference work on Anglo-Saxon history and with many interesting sidelights on culture and society; although quite old now, it remains the starting-point for historical writings on the period. Part of the "Oxford History of England" series.

Welch, M. *The English Heritage Book of Anglo-Saxon England* Batsford, 1992
Good archaeology-based guide to the early Anglo-Saxon period, many of the places can still be visited and the artefacts seen in museums across the country.

(b) Old English Literature

Alexander, M. *Old English Literature* Macmillan, 1983
A literary-historical tour through the better-known texts. Part of the "Macmillan History of Literature" series.

Brown, M. P. *Anglo-Saxon Manuscripts* British Library, 1991
Interesting small book on early manuscripts with many excellent illustrative reproductions of original manuscript pages.

Godden, M. and Lapidge, M. *The Cambridge Companion to Old English Literature* Cambridge, 1991
A fine collection of essays by experts in their various fields, dealing with most aspects of Old English language and literature. Although written for those without a detailed knowledge of the language, the standards of literary criticism will be most useful for those who have at least some familiarity with the texts.

Herbert, K. *Looking for the Lost Gods of England* Anglo-Saxon Books, 1994
A comprehensive and well-written introduction to the sources of our knowledge of the pre-Christian past.

—*Spellcraft – Old English Heroic Legends* Anglo-Saxon Books, 1993
An imaginative reconstruction of some of the heroic tales which were known to the early English by an accomplished novelist; supplemented by details of how these tales were pieced together from scattered references. Invaluable for anyone contemplating creative writing for the Anglo-Saxon period.

II. Old English Literature in Translation

(a) Prose

Garmonsway, G. N. *The Anglo-Saxon Chronicle* Everyman, 1972
Dense translation of the Chronicles (indicating and using various manuscripts) with explanatory notes. A book which will be especially prized by those with an interest in Anglo-Saxon history but no intention of learning the language.

Griffiths, B. *An Introduction to Early English Law* Anglo-Saxon Books, 1995
A useful introduction to the fundamental concepts underlying Anglo-Saxon law of various periods, avoiding the disputed technicalities of nomenclature.

(b) Verse

Alexander, M. *Beowulf* Penguin 1973
Very readable alliterative verse translation of the poem with much explanatory material, in the "Penguin Classics" series.

—*The Earliest English Poems* Penguin 1966
Good selection of Anglo-Saxon poetry turned into alliterative Modern English, with short but useful appendices on runes and Old English metre.

Crossley-Holland, K. *The Exeter Book Riddles* Penguin 1979
The "Penguin Classics" version of the Exeter Book with translations, solutions and notes.

Hamer, R. *A Choice of Anglo-Saxon Verse* Faber, 1970
One of the few books to give both the Old English text and a translation. Very useful for those who have begun studying the language but do not yet have the confidence to tackle texts unaided.

Porter, J. *Anglo-Saxon Riddles* Anglo-Saxon Books, 1995
Visually attractive selection of some of the more interesting riddles from the Exeter Book.

III. The Old English Language

(a) Language Courses

Davis, N. *Sweet's Anglo-Saxon Primer* Oxford (constantly reprinted since 1882)
An old-fashioned, traditional primer with a short grammar and selected Old English text excerpts.

Mitchell, B. and Robinson, F. C. *A Guide to Old English* Blackwell, 1968
Comprehensive guide to the language most suited to students working with a teacher, or with some experience of language studies.

Mitchell, B. *An Invitation to Old English and Anglo-Saxon England*, Blackwell, 1995
Building on the success of his collaborative work with Fred Robinson, this is Bruce Mitchell's own version of the *Guide* with much additional material relating to the history, material culture and civilization of the early English.

A language course called *First Steps in Old English* by Stephen Pollington is available from Anglo-Saxon Books. The author has adopted a step by step approach which enables students of differing abilities to advance at their own pace. There are many exercises designed to aid the learning process. A correspondence course and an audio tape of the author reading Old English texts is also available. For further details please see the back of this book.

(b) Reference Works

Clark-Hall, J. R. *A Concise Anglo-Saxon Dictionary* Toronto University Press, 1960

A useful and inexpensive reprint of a standard reference work.

Pollington, S. *Wordcraft. A Concise Dictionary and Thesaurus* Anglo-Saxon Books, 1993

The only easily available English to Old English dictionary, with themed vocabulary listings.

Whitelock, D. *Sweet's Anglo-Saxon Reader in Prose and Verse* Oxford, (constantly reprinted since 1967).

Classic selection of students' texts with notes and glossary.

IV. Place Name Studies

Cameron, K. *English Place-Names* Batsford, 1977

A brisk tour through place-name history.

Ekwall, E. *The Concise Oxford Dictionary of English Place-Names* Oxford, 1960

A handy alphabetical summary of the major place-names and their elements. A little dated, but still a good starting point for any further studies – packed with information.

Gelling, M. *Signposts to the Past.* Phillimore, 1988

Good, readable guide to the study of place-names, what they can tell us and how we can use that information.

Individual counties' place-names are published by the *English Place-Name Society* in volumes dealing in detail with the early records. Most English counties have now been covered. The *Introduction to the Survey* and *Chief Elements used in English Place-names* (i.e. the individual items of landscape vocabulary which recur) have been reprinted as a single volume. They are all available from the *EPNS* at Nottingham University, NG7 2RD.

Ælfric's Homily on Ascension day, part of a two-year course of sermons actually preached by him, in the vernacular, c.990.

Other Titles

Wordcraft: Concise English/Old English Dictionary and Thesaurus
Stephen Pollington

Wordcraft provides Old English equivalents to the commoner modern words in both dictionary and thesaurus formats. Previously the lack of an accessible guide to vocabulary deterred many would-be students of Old English. *Wordcraft* combines the core of indispensable words relating to everyday life with a selection of terms connected with society, culture, technology, religion, perception, emotion and expression to encompass all aspects of Anglo-Saxon experience. The Thesaurus presents vocabulary relevant to a wide range of individual topics in alphabetical lists, thus making it easily accessible to those with specific areas of interest. Each thematic listing is encoded for cross-reference from the Dictionary. The two sections will be of invaluable assistance to students of the language, as well as those with either a general or a specific interest in the Anglo-Saxon period.

£11·95   ISBN 1–898281–02–5   A5   256 pages

First Steps in Old English: An easy to follow language course for the beginner
Stephen Pollington

A complete, well presented and easy to use Old English language course that contains all the exercises and texts needed to learn Old English. This course has been designed to be of help to a wide range of students, from those who are teaching themselves at home, to undergraduates who are learning Old English as part of their English degree course. The author is aware that some individuals have little aptitude for learning languages and that many have difficulty with grammar. To help overcome these problems he has adopted a step by step approach that enables students of differing abilities to advance at their own pace. The course includes many exercises designed to aid the learning process. A correspondence course is also available.

£19   ISBN 1-898281-19-X   9½" x 6¼"/245 x 170mm   224 pages

Ærgeweorc: Old English Verse and Prose read by Stephen Pollington

This audiotape cassette can be used in conjunction with *First Steps in Old English* or just listened to for the sheer pleasure of hearing Old English spoken well.
Tracks: 1. Deor. 2. Beowulf – The Funeral of Scyld Scefing. 3. Engla Tocyme (The Arrival of the English). 4. Ines Domas. Two Extracts from the Laws of King Ine. 5. Deniga Hergung (The Danes' Harrying) Anglo-Saxon Chronicle Entry AD997. 6. Durham 7. The Ordeal (Be ðon ðe ordales weddigaþ) 8. Wið Dweorh (Against a Dwarf) 9. Wið Wennum (Against Wens) 10. Wið Wæterælfadle (Against Waterelf Sickness) 11. The Nine Herbs Charm 12. Læcedomas (Leechdoms) 13. Beowulf's Greeting 14. The Battle of Brunanburh 15. Blacmon – by Adrian Pilgrim.

£7·50   ISBN 1–898281–20–3   C40 audiotape

Peace-Weavers and Shield-Maidens: Women in Early English Society
Kathleen Herbert

The recorded history of the English people did not start in 1066 as popularly believed but one thousand years earlier. The Roman historian Cornelius Tacitus noted in *Germania*, published in the year 98, that the English (Latin *Anglii*), who lived in the southern part of the Jutland peninsula, were members of an alliance of Goddess-worshippers. The author has taken that as an appropriate opening to an account of the earliest Englishwomen, the part they played in the making of England, what they did in peace and war, the impressions they left in Britain and on the continent, how they were recorded in the chronicles, how they come alive in heroic verse and jokes.

£4·95   ISBN 1–898281–11–4   A5   64 pages

A Guide to Late Anglo-Saxon England: From Alfred to Eadgar II 871–1074
Donald Henson

This guide has been prepared with the aim of providing the general readers with both an overview of the period and a wealth of background information. Facts and figures are presented in a way that makes this a useful reference handbook.

Contents include: The Origins of England; Physical Geography; Human Geography; English Society; Government and Politics; The Church; Language and Literature; Personal Names; Effects of the Norman Conquest. All of the kings from Alfred to Eadgar II are dealt with separately and there is a chronicle of events for each of their reigns. There are also maps, family trees and extensive appendices.

£12·95 ISBN 1–898281–21–1 9½" x 6¾"/245 x 170mm, 6 maps & 3 family trees 208 pages

The English Warrior from earliest times to 1066
Stephen Pollington

This is not intended to be a bald listing of the battles and campaigns from the Anglo-Saxon Chronicle and other sources, but rather it is an attempt to get below the surface of Anglo-Saxon warriorhood and to investigate the rites, social attitudes, mentality and mythology of the warfare of those times.

The book is divided into three main sections that deal with warriorhood, weaponry and warfare respectively. The first covers the warrior's role in early English society, his rights and duties, the important rituals of feasting, gift giving and duelling, and the local and national military organizations. The second part discusses the various weapons and items of military equipment which are known to have been in use during the period, often with a concise summary of the generally accepted typology for the many kinds of military hardware. In the third part, the social and legal nature of warfare is presented, as well as details of strategy and tactics, military buildings and earthworks, and the use of supply trains. Valuable appendices offer original translations of the three principal Old English military poems, the battles of *Maldon*, *Finnsburh* and *Brunanburh*.

The latest thinking from many disciplines is brought together in a unique and fascinating survey of the role of the military in Anglo-Saxon England. The author combines original translations from the Old English and Old Norse source documents with archaeological and linguistic evidence to present a comprehensive and wide-ranging treatment of the subject. Students of military history will find here a wealth of new insights into a neglected period of English history.

This new edition has been updated and expanded.

£14·95 ISBN 1–898281–27–0 9½" x 6¾"/245 x 170mm over 50 illustrations 288 pages

Leechcraft: Early English Charms, Plantlore and Healing
Stephen Pollington

An unequalled examination of every aspect of early English healing, including the use of plants, amulets, charms, and prayer. Other topics covered include Anglo-Saxon witchcraft; tree-lore; gods, elves and dwarves.

The author has brought together a wide range of evidence for the English healing tradition, and presented it in a clear and readable manner. The extensive 2,000-entry index makes it possible for the reader to quickly find specific information.

The three key Old English texts are reproduced in full, accompanied by new translations.

Bald's Third Leechbook; *Lacnunga*; *Old English Herbarium*.

£35 ISBN 1–898281–23–8 10" x 6¾" (254 x 170mm) hardcover 28 illustrations 544 pages

Looking for the Lost Gods of England
Kathleen Herbert

Kathleen Herbert sifts through the royal genealogies, charms, verse and other sources to find clues to the names and attributes of the Gods and Goddesses of the early English. The earliest account of English heathen practices reveals that they worshipped the Earth Mother and called her Nerthus. The tales, beliefs and traditions of that time are still with us and able to stir our minds and imaginations.

£4·95 ISBN 1–898281–04–1 A5 64 pages

A Handbook of Anglo-Saxon Food: Processing and Consumption
Ann Hagen

For the first time information from various sources has been brought together in order to build up a picture of how food was grown, conserved, prepared and eaten during the period from the beginning of the 5th century to the 11th century. No specialist knowledge of the Anglo-Saxon period or language is needed, and many people will find it fascinating for the views it gives of an important aspect of Anglo-Saxon life and culture. In addition to Anglo-Saxon England the Celtic west of Britain is also covered. Subject headings include: drying, milling and bread making; dairying; butchery; preservation and storage; methods of cooking; meals and mealtimes; fasting; feasting; food shortages and deficiency diseases.

£9·95 ISBN 0–9516209–8–3 A5 192 pages

A Second Handbook of Anglo-Saxon Food & Drink
Production & Distribution
Ann Hagen

This second handbook complements the first and brings together a vast amount of information. Subject headings include: cereal crops; vegetables, herbs and fungi; fruit and nuts; cattle; sheep; goats; pigs; poultry and eggs; wild animals and birds; honey; fish and molluscs; imported food; tabooed food; provision of a water supply; fermented drinks; hospitality and charity. 27-page index.

Food production for home consumption was the basis of economic activity throughout the Anglo-Saxon period and ensuring access to an adequate food supply was a constant preoccupation. Used as payment and a medium of trade, food was the basis of the Anglo-Saxons' system of finance and administration.

£14·95 ISBN 1–898281–12–2 A5 432 pages

Anglo-Saxon Riddles
Translated by John Porter

This is a book full of ingenious characters who speak their names in riddles. Here you will meet a one-eyed garlic seller, a bookworm, an iceberg, an oyster, the sun and moon and a host of others from the everyday life and imagination of the Anglo-Saxons.

John Porter's sparkling translations retain all the vigour and subtly of the original Old English poems, transporting us back over a thousand years to the roots of our language and literature.

This edition contains all 95 riddles of the Exeter Book.

£4·95 ISBN 1–898281–13–0 A5 112 pages

Ordering

Payment may be made by Visa, or Mastercard. Telephone orders accepted.
Payment may also be made by a cheque drawn on a UK bank in sterling.
If you are paying by cheque please make it payable to Anglo-Saxon Books and enclose it with your order. When ordering by post please write clearly.
UK deliveries add 10% up to a maximum of £2·50
Europe – including **Republic of Ireland** - add 10% plus £1 – all orders sent airmail
North America add 10% surface delivery, 30% airmail
Elsewhere add 10% surface delivery, 40% airmail
Overseas surface delivery 6–8 weeks; airmail 5–10 days
>   For a full list of titles and details of our North American distributor see our website at: www.asbooks.co.uk or send a s.a.e. to:

Anglo-Saxon Books

Frithgarth, Thetford Forest Park, Hockwold-cum-Wilton, Norfolk IP26 4NQ England

Tel: +44 (0)1842 828430 Fax: +44 (0)1842 828332

e-mail: sales@asbooks.co.uk

Þa Engliscan Gesiðas

Þa Engliscan Gesiðas (The English Companions) is a historical and cultural society exclusively devoted to Anglo-Saxon history. Its aims are to bridge the gap between scholars and non-experts, and to bring together all those with an interest in the Anglo-Saxon period, its language, culture and traditions, so as to promote a wider interest in, and knowledge of all things Anglo-Saxon. The Fellowship publishes a journal, *Widowinde,* which helps members to keep in touch with current thinking on topics from art and archaeology to heathenism and Early English Christianity. The Fellowship enables like-minded people to keep in contact by publicising conferences, courses and meetings that might be of interest to its members.
>   For further details see www.kami.demon.co.uk/gesithas/ or write to: The Membership Secretary, Þa Engliscan Gesiðas, BM Box 4336, London, WC1N 3XX England.

Regia Anglorum

Regia Anglorum is a society that was founded to accurately re-create the life of the British people as it was around the time of the Norman Conquest. Our work has a strong educational slant and we consider authenticity to be of prime importance. We prefer, where possible, to work from archaeological materials and are extremely cautious regarding such things as the interpretation of styles depicted in manuscripts. Approximately twenty-five per cent of our membership, of over 500 people, are archaeologists or historians.

The Society has a large working Living History Exhibit, teaching and exhibiting more than twenty crafts in an authentic environment. We own a forty-foot wooden ship replica of a type that would have been a common sight in Northern European waters around the turn of the first millennium AD. Battle re-enactment is another aspect of our activities, often involving 200 or more warriors.
>   For further information see www.regia.org or contact: K. J. Siddorn, 9 Durleigh Close, Headley Park, Bristol BS13 7NQ, England, e-mail: kim_siddorn@compuserve.com

West Stow Anglo-Saxon Village

An early Anglo-Saxon Settlement reconstructed on the site where it was excavated consisting of timber and thatch hall, houses and workshop. Open all year 10am–4.15pm (except Yule). Special provision for school parties. A teachers' resource pack is available. Costumed events are held at weekends, especially Easter Sunday and August Bank Holiday Monday. Craft courses are organised.

> For further details see www.stedmunds.co.uk/west_stow.html or contact:
> The Visitor Centre, West Stow Country Park, Icklingham Road, West Stow,
> Bury St Edmunds, Suffolk IP28 6HG Tel: 01284 728718

Bede's World at Jarrow

Bede's world tells the remarkable story of the life and times of the Venerable Bede, 673–735 AD. Visitors can explore the origins of early medieval Northumbria and Bede's life and achievements through his own writings and the excavations of the monasteries at Jarrow and other sites.

Location – 10 miles from Newcastle upon Tyne, off the A19 near the southern entrance to the River Tyne tunnel. Bus services 526 & 527

> Bede's World, Church Bank, Jarrow, Tyne and Wear, NE32 3DY
> Tel: 0191 489 2106; Fax: 0191 428 2361; website: www.bedesworld.co.uk

Sutton Hoo near Woodbridge, Suffolk

Sutton Hoo is a group of low burial mounds overlooking the River Deben in south-east Suffolk. Excavations in 1939 brought to light the richest burial ever discovered in Britain – an Anglo-Saxon ship containing a magnificent treasure which has become one of the principal attractions of the British Museum. The mound from which the treasure was dug is thought to be the grave of Rædwald, an early English king who died in 624/5 AD.

THE SITE IS OPEN TO VISITORS FOR GUIDED TOURS ONLY

Weekend tours – Guided tours start at the site at 2pm and 3pm every Saturday, Sunday and Bank Holiday Monday from Easter Saturday until the end of September. There is no need to book, just turn up for the tour. Each tour lasts between 45 minutes and an hour, and brings to life the history and archaeology of the burial site and the story of its excavation.

Access by foot only – one mile walk along a footpath from the B1083. Tours can be booked at other times for organised parties. For details write to:-

> The Sutton Hoo Visits and Guiding Secretary, Tailor's House, Bawdsey, Woodbridge,
> Suffolk IP12 3AJ; e-mail: visits@suttonhoo.org; website: www.suttonhoo.org

The Sutton Hoo Society

Our aims and objectives focus on promoting research and education relating to the Anglo Saxon Royal cemetery at Sutton Hoo, Suffolk in the UK. The Society publishes a newsletter SAXON twice a year, which keeps members up to date with society activities, carries resumes of lectures and visits, and reports progress on research and publication associated with the site. If you would like to join the Society please write to:

> Membership Secretary, Sutton Hoo Society,
> 258 The Pastures, High Wycombe, Buckinghamshire HP13 5RS England
> website: www.suttonhoo.org